A Top Pot

Explorer Challenge

What happens to Dad's pot?

OXFORD
UNIVERSITY PRESS

Chip went to Top Pots.

Chip got a ball of clay.

Chip had a pot.

Chip got a bit of clay.

Chip got it to fit on top of his pot.

Chip put black bits on his pot.

Chip had a panda pot.

Retell the Story

Look at the pictures and retell the story in your own words.

Look Back, Explorers

What was Chip's pot made out of?

How did Chip make his pot?

What animal did the pot look like in the end?

Did you find out what happened to Dad's pot?

Explorer Challenge: it fell over (page 7)

What's Next, Explorers?

Now read about pots and lots of things made from different materials ...

Spot the Pot

Catherine Baker
Series created by Roderick Hunt and Alex Brychta

OXFORD

Explorer Challenge
for *Spot the Pot*

What is this made of?